A FIRST AMERICANS BOOK
THE SEMINOLES

Virginia Driving Hawk Sneve   Illustrated by Ronald Himler

HOLIDAY HOUSE · NEW YORK

A NOTE FROM THE PUBLISHER

The Seminoles was first published in 1994. To update and prepare the book for republication today, we have worked with the Ah-Tah-Thi-Ki Museum, the official museum of the Seminole Tribe of Florida, and with Donald L. Fixico (Shawnee, Sac and Fox, Muscogee Creek, and Seminole), Regents and Distinguished Foundation Professor of History at Arizona State University. We hope this book serves as an introduction to one of the first American Nations and that you will continue to explore Seminole history and culture by visiting the websites listed in the back of the book.

ACKNOWLEDGMENTS

The quotations from Osceola, Coacoochee, Neamathla, and Holata Micco are from *The Origin, Progress, and Conclusion of the Florida War* by John T. Sprague, D. Appleton Co., New York, 1848.

The Joe Dan Osceola quotations are from *Osceola: The Unconquered Indian* by William and Ellen Hartley; Hawthorn Books, Inc.; New York, 1973.

Text copyright © 1994, 2024 by Virginia Driving Hawk Sneve
Illustrations copyright © 1994 by Ronald Himler
All Rights Reserved
HOLIDAY HOUSE is registered in the U.S. Patent and Trademark Office.
Printed and bound in August 2024 at Toppan Leefung, DongGuan, China.
www.holidayhouse.com
Second Edition
3 5 7 10 8 6 4 2

The Library of Congress has catalogued the prior edition as follows:

Sneve, Virginia Driving Hawk.
The Seminoles / Virginia Driving Hawk Sneve; illustrated by Ronald Himler
p. cm. – (A First Americans Book)
Summary: Discusses the history, lifestyle, customs, and current situation of the Seminoles.
ISBN: 0-8234-1112-5
1. Seminole Indians – Juvenile literature. [1. Seminole Indians. 2. Indians of North America.]
I. Himler, Ronald, ill. II. Title. III. Series: Sneve, Virginia Driving Hawk. First Americans book.
E99.S28S64   1994   93-14316   CIP   AC
305.897'3 – dc20

Second Edition
ISBN: 978-0-8234-5858-5 (hardcover)
ISBN: 978-0-8234-6093-9 (paperback)

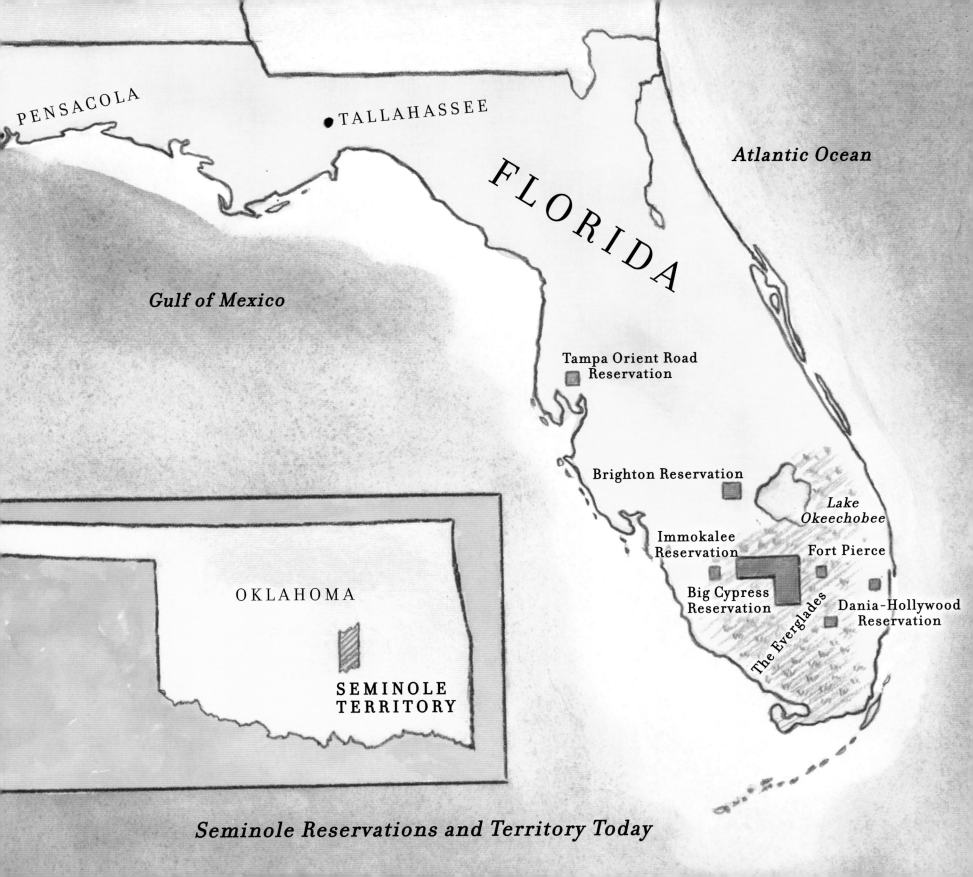

PENSACOLA

• TALLAHASSEE

Atlantic Ocean

F L O R I D A

Gulf of Mexico

Tampa Orient Road
Reservation

Brighton Reservation

*Lake
Okeechobee*

Immokalee
Reservation

Fort Pierce

OKLAHOMA

Big Cypress
Reservation

The Everglades

Dania-Hollywood
Reservation

SEMINOLE
TERRITORY

Seminole Reservations and Territory Today

Muscogee Seminole Creation Story

A long time ago, the world was in darkness. There was a veil of water over the earth, like a mist, and no one could see. The Muscogees emerged from the earth, like they were emerging from a cave onto the surface of the earth, and they held hands as they could not see. But then a light breeze came and blew the mist away, and for the first time, like the dawn of a new day, the people could see the earth, and all the animals too.

So this is why the Wind is important as one of the four elemental powers with Fire, Water, and Earth, and why animals became the totems of the people.

The First Seminoles

Why cannot we live here in peace?
COACOOCHEE (WILDCAT)

Muscogee leader

The history of the Seminoles begins with the first people of Florida, their ancestors, who came to the region more than fourteen thousand years ago. Before the Spanish and other colonizers arrived, native people moved throughout the southeast, what is today known as Florida, Georgia, Alabama, and other states. States did not exist then, so people moved freely and interacted with each other over many generations. When colonial forces came, they disrupted this way of life. They named groups of Indians and tried to keep them in certain areas. For example, there were groups of Indians that lived along streams in what are now southern Georgia and Alabama. In about 1708, white men came to this country and mistakenly called these Indians "Creeks" because of where they lived. The white men drove the Muscogees away from the streams and took their land. To escape the white men, a group of Indians moved south to territory that later became northern Florida and settled around what is now Tallahassee. The Muscogees called this group "Seminoles," which has been translated as "runaways" or "separatists," but has also been interpreted to mean "lovers of freedom" or "lovers of the wilds." The Seminoles did not want to live among white people or with other Indians who accepted the white men's way of life. This group joined other indigenous people in Florida. All eventually became known as Seminoles.

Burial mounds found on Florida's west coast show that Indians were in the area fourteen thousand years ago. In the 1500s, the Spanish, the first white men to come to Florida, found more than ten thousand Timucua Indians living there. The Spanish tried to convert and enslave these Indians, killing many of them. The remaining people joined with groups of Indians who eventually became Seminole.

In northern Florida, these ancestors farmed the rich land and raised horses and cattle they had gotten from the Spanish. The men hunted wild game, and the women made pottery.

These people built large dugout canoes, sturdy enough for ocean voyages. They often traveled across the Gulf of Mexico and went as far south as Cuba and the Bahamas. Their knowledge and experience would later help them make a home in the Everglades, a large swampy area in southern Florida.

The Seminole War

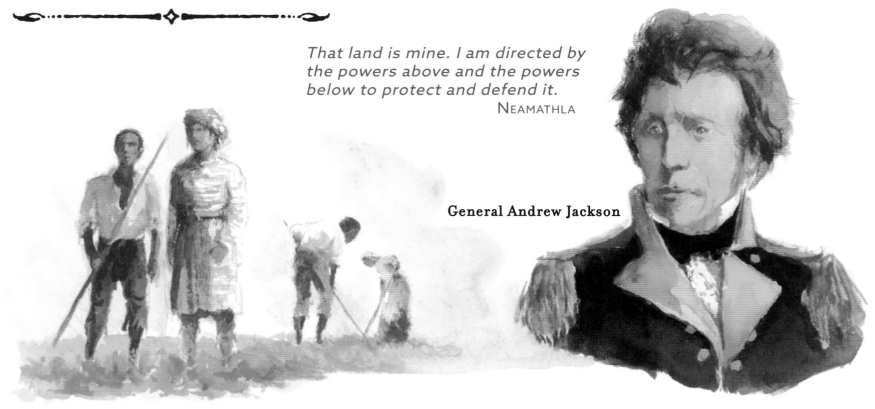

That land is mine. I am directed by the powers above and the powers below to protect and defend it.
NEAMATHLA

General Andrew Jackson

In 1800, Spain claimed Florida, and this put the Seminoles under Spanish laws. Like the white men, the Seminoles had Black slaves, but they were not bought and sold like property. Some slaves became free and joined Seminole forces as their allies. This alarmed the U.S. government.

In 1814, General Andrew Jackson attacked Creek villages in Georgia to get more land for the white settlers. Many Muscogees fled to their Seminole relatives in Florida. Among them were a young woman and her son, Osceola, who would grow up to become a great Seminole leader.

The white men who took the Muscogees' farms wanted their runaway slaves in Florida to be returned. The Seminoles refused to give back these slaves, so the government of Georgia sent troops to hunt them down. Only a few were caught.

Since the Seminoles had sided with England during the Revolutionary War (1775–1883), the U.S. government already thought of the Seminoles as enemies. During the War of 1812, fought between the United States and England, Spain allowed English ships to be based in Pensacola. The United States government sent General Andrew Jackson to Florida, where he raided Muscogee and Seminole villages to keep the Indians from fighting on the side of England. After the war, even though Seminole land was still Spanish territory, white settlers moved into Florida to claim it.

While the U.S. government referred to the first, second, and third Seminole Wars, to the indigenous people who experienced it, the entire period was one long war. Hostilities continued during the supposed peace times in between the official first, second, and third part.

The War Continues

We were all made by the same great Father and are like his children.
HOLATA MICCO

In 1819, Spain sold Florida to the United States. Slave catchers from Georgia and other southern states came to reclaim the slaves who had escaped earlier. The owners not only caught former slaves, but they also took Black people who had been born free in Florida, and even captured mixed-blood and full-blood Seminoles. The Indians and Black people who escaped fled into the swamps.

In 1823, the Seminoles signed a treaty called the Treaty of Moultrie Creek, giving up most of their land. They had to leave the good farming country of north Florida and move into a reservation in the central part of the state. Despite the government's promise that the Seminoles would be safe from attacks if they obeyed U.S. laws, they were not safe. More settlers were moving into Florida and wanted Seminole land. They attacked the Indians and destroyed their crops.

Seminoles being attacked by white soldiers

The settlers wanted the Seminoles to be moved out of Florida. In 1828, Andrew Jackson, now president of the United States, signed the Indian Removal Act of 1830 that required all Indians in the southeastern United States to be removed to the Indian Territory, which later became the state of Oklahoma.

The majority of the Seminoles refused to go. They did not want to leave their families and homes. Although the U.S. military sent twelve generals to Florida to try to defeat the Seminoles and even used bloodhounds to track them, for seven years the Seminoles resisted by striking at the white soldiers, then vanishing into the swamps where the enemy could not follow. The U.S. government called this the Second Seminole War.

Osceola and Wildcat

*I say we must not leave
our homes and lands!*
OSCEOLA

Coacoochee (Wildcat)

Osceola

Warriors such as Coacoochee (Wildcat) and Osceola became the most famous Native Americans in the world. Osceola met with U.S. government officials in April 1835. The officials tried to persuade the Seminoles to leave, but Osceola refused to sign the agreement. Instead, he pulled out his knife and stabbed it through the paper, showing that he would rather fight than leave Florida. His people were hiding in the swamps where they were safe.

Coacoochee was a Florida Seminole who was also concerned with the safety of his people. He led Seminole warriors and their allies in fights with the United States Army.

In 1836, Osceola and other followers were persuaded to meet with army officers to discuss peace terms. They met with the officers under a white flag, but instead of talking about peace, the soldiers arrested the Indians and two Black Seminoles and imprisoned them at Fort Marion in Florida. Osceola and his men refused to eat. They fasted for six days until they were thin enough to squeeze through the prison bars and escape.

Osceola and Coacoochee (Wildcat) being taken prisoner

Osceola was ill at Fort Marion and stayed a prisoner. In 1837, Osceola and his family were taken to Fort Moultrie, South Carolina, where the great leader died one year later.

Now the Seminole tribe was divided. Some surrendered and moved to Fort Gibson in the Indian Territory. Hundreds of this group died on the journey to Indian Territory from illness, poor food, bad weather, and exhaustion. Those who made it to Fort Gibson received supplies to move on again to their designated Seminole reservation.

Wildcat became the leader of the Seminole bands that stayed in Florida. They hid deep in the Everglades where they could not be found. They appeared suddenly to fight the U.S. soldiers, then just as suddenly vanished into the swamps.

After Wildcat's daughter was taken captive by the U.S. Army, Wildcat was finally persuaded to surrender. In 1841, Wildcat, with his band of Black and Seminole warriors and their families, was removed to Oklahoma. But when the U.S. government made plans to enslave the Black Seminoles in Wildcat's band, he escaped and went to Mexico. The Mexican government gave him and his followers land in exchange for their guarding the border against the Americans. The Seminoles who stayed in Florida isolated themselves in the Everglades.

Life in the Everglades

chickees

The Seminoles in Florida explored every part of the Everglades by traveling over the swampy waterways in dugout canoes. They quickly adapted to this swampland, called a "river of grass" because of the tall, sharp-edged saw grass that grew in the water. The Everglades covered an area one hundred miles long and seventy miles wide from Lake Okeechobee to the Gulf of Mexico.

Scattered throughout the Everglades were hammocks, dry islands or mounds with trees and rich soil. The Seminoles found that they were good, safe places to live because few white men ventured near them.

Not only did the Everglades protect the Seminoles, but its dense forests provided shelter. The Indians erected *chickees*, open houses thatched with palmetto leaves, that stood about three feet off the ground. The slanting roof gave protection from the sun and rain, and the chickee was pleasantly cool and dry.

The Seminoles planted gardens in the fertile hammock soil. They grew sweet potatoes, pumpkins, melons, and corn, their most important crop.

From the corn, the women made *sofkee*, a drink that was a favorite dish. Another favorite was bread made of *coontie* flour, which was made from the ground-up roots of the coontie plant. If not washed and prepared in the right way, the flour from this root would be poisonous.

Seminole women wove baskets from the palmetto stalks that grew in the swamp. They also had knives, iron pots and kettles, and metal garden hoes.

Each family did its cooking over a big open fire in the center of the village. This fire burned day and night.

Skilled Hunters and Traders

The people in council have agreed. By their chiefs, they have uttered.
OSCEOLA

Seminole hunter with blowgun

The Seminole men were responsible for defending their people. An especially brave man earned the title of *hadjo*. The leader of each town or village was a *micco*, or chief. The chiefs could appoint a war chief called *tustenuggee*.

Game was plentiful, and the Seminole men were skilled hunters. They had gotten guns from the Spanish, but after they moved into the Everglades, ammunition was difficult to find. Instead, they snared turkey, ducks, quail, and small game like rabbits and squirrels. If necessary, they could hunt with a blowgun made from a stalk of cane and darts made from shells or wood.

When the Seminoles hunted deer or bear without a gun, they used a long bow made from hickory. They fashioned arrowheads from the iron or brass they had gotten from the Spanish. They always retrieved the arrowhead after a kill because the metal was hard to get. When they had to, they used arrowheads made from shell or fish bone.

The Seminoles, like other tribes, had no money, but traded for the things they did not have. The Everglades was filled with alligators, otters, and birds with colorful feathers. The white men brought bees from Europe, and swarms escaped and found shelter in the swamps. The Indians made use of the honey and beeswax. They traded hides, bird pelts and plumage, honey, and wax to the white men for ammunition, beads, metal, and cloth. The Seminoles continued to trade into the early twentieth century.

Clothing

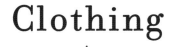

I asked but for a small piece of these lands, enough to plant and live upon . . .
COACOOCHEE

"flat roll" hairstyle

The Seminoles dressed differently from other southern Indians such as the Muscogees and Choctaws. The style of their clothes was influenced by Spanish cotton garments that were more comfortable than buckskin in the warm Florida climate.

The women made cool, loose-fitting clothes for their families. They wore long skirts and cape-like blouses. The men's shirts reached their knees. Both men and women wore leather moccasins and leggings to protect their feet and legs from the sharp grass and spiny plants found in the Everglades.

After the women acquired sewing machines in the late 1800s, they made bright patchwork designs that they sewed into colorful clothing. The women wore necklaces made of several strands of beads. The necklaces looked like a collar around their necks. The women combed their long hair into a wide, flat roll on the top of their heads. The men wore turbans and bandanas.

You're a Seminole and you come from the heritage of Osceola. That's what we tell our children . . .
JOE DAN OSCEOLA

Girls spent most of their time with older females and learned how to weave baskets, cook, and sew. Their dresses were not as elaborate as the women's. Older girls cared for toddlers, who often wore nothing at all.

The boys wore long shirts until they were old enough to learn to hunt. Then they dressed like the men. A boy was trained by his mother's brother to be a hunter and warrior.

The children had the responsibility of watching over the village fields. During the day, the children drove away the crows and other birds before they could eat the freshly sown seeds. After the plants grew, older boys stayed by the gardens all night to keep the raccoons and deer from eating the crops.

The children belonged to their mother's clan. A clan was named after a certain animal, a plant, or the wind. A clan was a group of people of the same clan animal, clan plant, or wind clan. A man who got married usually lived with his wife's clan. Children became members of their mother's clan.

Ceremony

The Seminoles believed that everything has a spirit and must be respected. It was a sacred responsibility to take care of the land that made their lives possible. The Seminoles passed down legends that explain the ways people should live in harmony with nature.

The Seminoles were grateful for the good life they found in the Everglades. They knew that the animals, birds, and plants made their life possible. They never took more than the people needed. They showed their respect and gratitude by taking clan names from the Panther, Otter, Wildcat, Wolf, Bear, Deer, Big Town (Toad), Bird, Snake, Alligator, and Wind.

Green Corn Dance

I can go to the Green Corn Dance, which is my Seminole ritual. I appreciate this, and I hope my children will do the same.
JOE DAN OSCEOLA

The clans came together once a year to celebrate the Green Corn Dance. It took place when it was time for the corn to ripen. The elders of the clans also met to settle disputes and discuss tribal concerns. Few non-Indians have seen a Green Corn Dance. Most Native Americans have a similar ceremony each year, where the Creator is thanked for providing food.

At the Green Corn Dance, Seminoles participate in different ceremonies. Men and women separate into different "camps" according to their clans. In earlier times, the Green Corn Dance marked an important occasion when Seminoles from different camps and areas would get together.

The gathering will include hours and hours of "stomp dancing," the single file style of dancing traditional to Seminole Indians. Following behind a chanting medicine man, or "leader," a string of male dancers will respond to each chant while women dancers quietly shuffle with them, providing the rhythm with shakers tied to their legs. The Green Corn Dance is held each spring. It takes place at various undisclosed locations in South Florida and few non-Indians have ever seen it.

The Seminole Nation

The white man says I shall go, and he will send people to make me go . . .
OSCEOLA

Seminole council house,
Wewoka, Indian Territory

The Seminoles who had to leave Florida took the Green Corn Dance ceremony with them in the 1830s to Indian Territory, which became the state of Oklahoma in 1907. They lived for a while with the Muscogees who had been removed from Georgia. Finally, in 1845, land was set aside for the Seminoles, but it wasn't until 1856 that the Seminole Nation in Indian Territory was established. There were twenty towns in the Seminole Nation, and its capital was at Wewoka, Indian Territory.

The Seminoles in the West lived off the land as their Florida relatives did in the Everglades. After oil was discovered in Seminole lands, only those Seminoles who had remained landowners benefited. Today, some of the Seminoles are farmers, and others are teachers or attorneys or work in other professions.

The Seminole War, the Third Part

Bolek (Billy Bowlegs)

What we had was a tremendous determination to fight for the things we believed in—in our freedom, in our land.
JOE DAN OSCEOLA

The Seminoles in Florida continued to be harassed by white settlers. The U.S. government kept up its efforts to move them to Indian Territory. In 1855, Bolek, chief of the clans who stayed in Florida, led the Seminoles in a third war against the white settlers. The whites thought "Bolek" sounded like "bowleg," so they called him Billy Bowlegs. Bolek and his warriors fought for three years until the U.S. government offered to pay the Seminoles to leave. But only Billy Bowlegs and 123 others left for Indian Territory.

The Seminoles who remained in Florida earned the name "the people who never surrendered" during the last part of the Seminole War.

The Seminoles Today

I never wish to tread upon my land unless I am free.
COACOOCHEE

The Florida Seminoles never signed a formal peace treaty with the United States. Up to the 1920s, the Seminoles still lived by hunting, fishing, and farming. Over the years, the Seminoles divided into two groups: the Seminole Tribe of Florida and the Muscogee Tribe of Indians of Florida.

The Seminole Tribe of Florida, Inc., has its headquarters on a reservation in Hollywood, Florida. The Tribe has other reservations in Florida where Seminole people live, including Big Cypress, Brighton, Immokalee, and Fort Pierce.

The "river of grass" is no longer as abundant or as large as it once was. The Seminoles can no longer survive living off the bounty of the Everglades. Much of the swampland has been filled with land and covered with the suburban homes of Florida's cities.

Today, the Seminole Tribe of Florida provides many services to its people, including schools, libraries, health care, and police. Many run businesses, work in offices, and become artists. They also become doctors, lawyers, and politicians. Some raise cattle and work as cowboys. Some become ministers and work in churches. Some wrestle alligators and perform for tourists. In 1979, the Florida Seminoles introduced tribal bingo after their leaders observed a Catholic church hosting bingo games. Other tribes saw the Florida Seminoles making money, and this led to the Indian gaming industry based on gambling. Today, some Seminoles in both Florida and Oklahoma work in the casinos and restaurants that are owned by the Tribe.

In Oklahoma, at its tribal capital at Wewoka, the Seminoles offer their members health services, community services, and educational assistance. Both the Oklahoma and Florida Seminoles retain an awareness of the sacredness of the land and teach their children the responsibility of caring for it. Few Seminoles depend on farming for survival, but they still celebrate the Green Corn Dance to cleanse and renew their lives. It is a sacred ritual and is not open to the public. The Seminoles remember that they are still one people who shared a sacred fire.

The Great Spirit has given me legs to walk over the earth, hands to aid myself; eyes to see its ponds, rivers, forests, and game; then a head with which I think. The sun shines to warm us and bring forth our crops, and the moon brings back the spirits of our warriors, our fathers, wives, and children. Why can not we live here in peace?

COACOOCHEE

SandyShusterPhotography/Shutterstock

Dancers perform at the Seminole Tribal Fair and Powwow in south Florida.

EQRoy/Shutterstock

Some Seminoles today make a living working in Florida's tourism industry.

Sunshower Shots/Shutterstock

The Seminole Tribe of Florida owns Hard Rock International and operates the Seminole Hard Rock Hotel & Casino, located on eighty-seven acres of the Hollywood Seminole Reservation, Florida.

Seminole doll made by Mary Billie on the Big Cypress Reservation, Florida. Some Seminoles continue practicing cultural crafts passed down from generation to generation.

The First Americans Museum presents histories and cultures of all thirty-nine Native American tribes in Oklahoma, including the Seminole Nation of Oklahoma. This section of the OKLA HOMMA exhibit displays pop culture objects that misrepresent Indigenous people and explains how these stereotypes are harmful.

Young Seminole children play stick ball, long a Seminole tradition, on the Big Cypress Reservation, Florida.

FOR MORE INFORMATION ON THE SEMINOLES

The Seminole Tribe of Florida:
www.semtribe.com

The Seminole Nation of Oklahoma:
https://www.sno-nsn.org

The Ah-Tah-Thi-Ki Museum, Florida:
https://www.ahtahthiki.com

The Seminole Nation Museum, Oklahoma:
https://seminolenationmuseum.org

Seminole Doll Making, Florida:
https://www.floridamemory.com/learn/classroom/learning-units/seminole-dolls/photos/

The Seminole Tribune, Official Newspaper of the Seminole Tribe of Florida:
https://seminoletribune.org

Native Hope, "Seminole Nation: The Unconquered People":
https://blog.nativehope.org/seminole-nation-the-unconquered-people

MORE RESOURCES ABOUT NATIVE AMERICANS

Indigenous Photograph:
https://indigenousphotograph.com

Native American tribe websites:
https://libguides.du.edu/c.php?g=90322&p=582788

The National Museum of the American Indian:
https://americanindian.si.edu

Indian Country Today:
https://ictnews.org